# MOLESKINE #1: 33 SELECTED POEMS

colvet

Colvet

## Table of Contents

1. Heatwaves Rising
2. banjo boys @ the local
3. Redfield
4. Ode to Celestine Prophecy
5. Biases
6. $25 Life Lesson
7. Face Transplant (for a distorted face)
8. personalized medicine
9. question #1
10. Biotic Balls
11. seed * bear * bush
12. untitled #1
13. Hammer City
14. untitled #2
15. untitled #3
16. question #2
17. DELUSION//ILLUSION
18. April 2019 (written June 2019)
19. Creationary
20. a hospital type affair
21. Procession
22. Removal
23. [aqueous daydream]
24. a type of mom, I wish for #1 (Daggerfall)
25. out girl scouting
26. Dishonest Dissonance
27. A Filtration System
28. Bending Physics
29. den of inquiry
30. it's ashing
31. TAN
32. Pickering Fractals
33. {conditional string}

Moleskine #1: 33 Selected Poems

**i love you.**

**i hate me.**

*Heatwaves Rising*

We can visualize

the heatwaves rise

above the tarmac

sundering below

but only when hot enough

to let the flowers grow

but this force

must still exist

even when it snows...

so where oh where

do the heatwaves go?

Carve away your skull

leave your brain matter exposed

you'll be quite impressed

by what we all

still

may never know

## *banjo boys @ the local*

I want to hear

that banjo

ting

that mandolin riffage

and bright country

swing

Americana or Bluegrass

it's all the same

heart-broken boys

evolved to men full of

shame

You captivate the essence

of toils

of troubles

of blessings

of life

But lest

we have not forgotten

why

our tears turn to wine

Colvet

or acid into rain

Please

Please

Please

Just let me hear

that banjo

RING!

## *Redfield*

Ever seen the glow?
From the fields
the fauna
the farms
in row?

Have you seen
a white light
sometimes yellowish in hue
emanate
from that which bears life?

The Peruvian soldiers
will not be pleased
with the power
you've managed
to muster up

The intuitions
coincidences
spiritual whirlwinds
will constantly
guide you home

No matter the gust
the intensity
the frequency
or barometric output...
your inner love
and beauty
so divine
is always guiding you
internally
to where you must be
spatially

Remain present
and view
each
single
opportunity
as it may come
undone

## *Ode to Celestine Prophecy*

Can

you

see

the strings

or fibers

of smoke

emanating

from

your

fingertips?

Ah,

yes...

you've

got

it

kiddo!

*Biases*

Never underestimate

the power of an eyeball

gravitating

repulsive

strong enough to spook the soul

surge the senses

awaken the psyche

and torture he

who bears thy name

A gateway?

Leading to the soul?

Rather a dumbwaiter

Only bringing you

the sloth

and the indulgence

you crave

We render images

at real-time speeds

but an outside observer

may be all we need

Biases always accrue.

## Twenty-five Dollar Life Lesson

I have a few friends

and many enemies

some of whom

are all the way down in

New Orleans

Green was his promise

Mike was his name

I swear

to

fucking

God

I ain't ever

falling

for that one

again...

If I see you

In French Quarters

or witness you

in the street

I'll stab you in the

neck

Moleskine #1: 33 Selected Poems

unless I see my $25 BACK!

## *Face Transplant (for a Distorted Face)*

Swooning

feeding

over apathetic eyes

a darkened mask

made of imperial wood

cast from the high seven

seas

Yet creativity

is harder than steel

its burrowing quicker

than a jack rabbit

in 90 degree heat

Melting inwardly

fusing to the skin beneath

like that Goosebumps episode

"Mommy, my mask won't

come off!"

That's the woe

and hardship

of a single-willed individual
constantly wearing
dread
fear
anxiety
death
on thy skin

NOthing is free
NO action is free
from discourse
or a slapshot
jerk of the shoulders
knuckle-pucked

Maybe
that's just it
we live too closely
to our suffering
Never vacationing on the coast
Always landlocked
city
urbanite
prisoner

Colvet

forever forced
to bear its weight

I'd rather
use some moisturizer
or wear it
like a patch on sleeve
I'd still get judged
typical
oh, I am prepared

but at least
my face
would still be mine
and my mom
might recognize me,
not my
guilt
regret
hatred
despondency
[     ]
...currently slip-stitched
into my maxillocranio-

FACE
FACE
FACE!

My face
is forever distorted
oh, I need you
paper and pen
for you work
wonders
on my pores
more so
than Aloe Vera itself...

I just wish
<the surgeon>
used invisible
degradable
sutures

*Personalized Medicine*

drugs

n'

alcohol

rather

love

n'

beauty … CLICHE

or

the warming touch

of your intellect

fill the voids

of my brain

of my heart

of my insecurities

more than my

favourite

self-help

book…

Start your journey now!

## *Question 1*

Can ideas

stick

to

your shirt

(from their suspension in air)

the

same way

burrs

or seeds

get stuck on us

when travelling,

circumnavigating

a blanketed

forested

area?

*Biotic Balls*

You say
your days bleed together

What happens
when the blood pools
into a month?

Beginning to coagulate
into hardened spheres
of scab
to be strung on some craft yarn
as a mediocre holiday reminder

Then the months continue to grow
isotropically
like an *in vitro* bioreactor
exponentially increasing in mass
proliferative
fibrous capsule formed

Weight so heavy
the biotic balls
bounce to the dingy basement floor

a single string

left resonating above

leaving deflated sacks

slumped and scattered

the deadened years

I've always sought to carve away

from my own flesh

No need to interfere

Scoop the carcasses up

into a tall black trash bag

wasted life

at least these endothelial bundles

didn't have to bear that pain

see pain

is weightless as air

that is if you are a mere observer

but to those who must endure

---------------

I wish you the best.

*seed \* bear \* bush*

I want to see

if my seed

my coating

will unfurl

unroll

de-case

germinate

sprout

or grow

No idea

if I'll become a tree

but feeling

like a moss

on a perfectly poured

concrete driveway

I'll likely

just get a trim

and get tangled up

suffocate

die

. . .

maybe I'm so volatile

I need more space to

explore

or maybe I was

always destined

to be

a bush

## Untitled #1

Searching

through your pearls

smell

those diseased/deceased

pluck them from the rest

with a rusty wrench

like an effervescent poppy

aesthetic

potency off again

finding teeth

in your spaghetti sauce

never had

that great resounding din

or as much

pleasure

as the pheromones

eluting

from my skin

## *Hammer City*

Blindly

swinging hammers

at the wall

of the Canadian Red Cross

since the paint

vivaciously

says to


Nothing

says Steeltown

Hammer City

more

than a pair of

shiners

painted in acrylic

or a

Hamilton Harley

to ride

## Untitled #2

Linseed oil

lathered wood

chewing up saffron flowers

paisley lapels

sewn in place

red-light district lipstick

hidden behind

a solemn lull

exemplary

to your personality

sad Chinese food

on a Tuesday afternoon

...      ...      ...

never settled my stomach much.

With parts of stars

still stuck in your teeth

after you ate up all the planets

and inhaled everything

fasting

wasting

withering away

Here,
I'll get you a toothpick.

Face drooping
like a bruised
bashed fruit
not feeling like strawberry today
How about you?

Penning in the parts
of your face
to make you seem
alive
while feeling death
most of the time
still more blending
required,
now coconut oil
or isopropanol?

## Untitled #3

THAT MOMENT
WHEN YOU REALIZE
TO BE MORE OF A
MAN
YOU'VE GOTTA BE
MORE LIKE YOUR MUM,
A     WO-MAN
YEAH,
MAN

## *Question #2*

Are
muscle
fibers
the ashes
or
the embers
or
the kindling
to the
fires of passion
to the
flames of love
forever
burning
within
our
weary
hearts?

*DELUSION///ILLUSION*
big
BIGGER
# BIGGEST
**best**

Let my insecurities evolve

chemically

socially

physically

but <u>swiftly</u>

So I may find

my inner rank

I know its unimportant

but it matters to me

**DELUSIONAL**

it seems

I'm sorry.

## April 2019 (Written in June 2019)

To live a life

to live a lie

yields time

forever opulent

See truth

bears no meaning

it possesses merely a name

to describe the questions

indebted, rooted in the brain

May we muster up a prose

or poetic resounding din

to resonate long enough

to let us be fulfilled?


Rather riddle me this

if we are those

sole mortals

responsible

for the firing squad

beratement

of

question

Colvet

have we really won?

I must know...
WHO IS HOLDING THE GUN?

Suicidal homicide
homicidal suicide
chronology
bears no witness
with enough wit
laughs
or cherubic charm
to ever place
the soul at ease

We are all living
we are all lying
therefore we are all
chaos
collectively
not consciously
so these pungent thoughts
may be only scabs
not unique
everlasting

Moleskine #1: 33 Selected Poems

thoughts

Riddling our brains
our lives
with stale
brown
blood

*Creationary*
Intellectualism
favours matter over mind
but rather
must both exist
to see the outward flow
extension
final piece application
to impact those
whom
we've always had in mind

A thought
no matter how profound
is useless
unless it may reach outward
anisotropically
stretching
and contorting
forever seeking
progression
and strengthening

If this may be true

Bergson, Henri
has cracked the final seal
of our psychological coffins
us scientists yearn
to gasp for air inside of
closeted
from _true_ reality
whatever that means

We've become fixated
even indebted
to our ability
rather
our default pilot mode
to constantly categorize
and place into little boxes
little boxes on the hillside

See emotion
noisy, blurring feelings
are reactive
to the celestial
even provoked
inner energy

Colvet

forever flowing
with the sway or tilt
of the sphere we call home

But us humans
know roughly
how to do the work-up
put on the finishing touches
to illuminate
our ever-present role
in the universe
to simply be
observe
reflect
and share said knowledge
whilst keeping our genetic underpinnings intact

For these
are the only
true visions of purpose
of man
or woman
wandering
in the electrically

buzzing
aftermath
of our own creation
and of our own demise

No matter what we know
or ought to know
or what we think we may have known
our battle
with the inefficacies of emotion
still persist
and their presence
may prelude to our next stage
of evolution

*a hospital type affair*
purposefully
placing
cigarette burns
singeing ends
on the fringe
of your old man's chair
tearing
ripping
faltering at the seams
pushing up lumpy
airy
fatigued foamy gunk
flowing
like a stream of nutrients and
beings
rather
harmonized dreams
from days and nights
forever long
basking in the daily
sun
unless its a depressed Mayan increment

when ones sits
and ruminates
letting the stress
and anxiety
drip from the skin
and it gets absorbed
underneath
filtering out the solids
from their liquid
carrying medium
settling
sedimenting
into the inner-workings
of this morose
furniture display
I wonder
if it works like LSD
when you crack your back too much
or are in a car accident
or get a tattoo
any vibration
really
if strong enough
can cause the caverns in your bones

to shift and to rumble
like an Indiana Jones movie
carving into the deep
dig dug
drawn
Earth
as stone breaks mud
and mud becomes dirt
causing the bats
to flee their nooks
and their crannied cramped homes
You feel the entire earth shake
and hear
a flowing
gushing
back-washed stream
glowing with a tinge of orange
goldenrod yellow
violently
and turbulently
filling
and flowing
through the porous voids
of your central nervous system

causing your brain to crack
like a plastic-wrapped
store bought
glow stick
toy
just one snap
one shake
one 15 seconds later
and BAM!
you have light
as I roll around in this chair
bending
and breaking my back
rolling my neck
spasming my muscles
I can smell that fear
and the destiny of a boy
lost away
in a kingdom far from home
there are no strewn Christmas lights
with letters
or words
for me to communicate
my mom was never that

Colvet

clever
she ain't a Ryder
but I think I feel
the cotton getting soaked
as the butterfly IV
flies away
and I'm left sitting
in my chair
well...
not my chair exactly
but still
functioning
all the same...
in a hospital
type
affair

## *Procession*

Deep in the plains
not the type in Ohio
one with a long stretch
of bigwig shoppes
and special services
bringing me farther
from the city

I just see hazard lights
from the window of the 101
Just two
Maybe people moving?
Now four
Possibly a government raid?
No 10
I'm panicking again

Just wait
there's the obsidian hearse
on guard at the frontline
with oblong windows
and residual oil buff
the gleam from the jet-black paint

Colvet

under the blaring sun
is contrasting to me
absorbing all of the photons
leaving a corpse in its place
on the very streets I navigate
to perform my {tax} duty
as an honest citizen

## *Removal*

Death as term
becomes colloquial
but our interpretations
as humans
differ
as I'm staring
and nodding
and pondering
I see what appears before me
A quintessential
Yet disastrous fate
That only I
may truly feel
eyes peeled back
only for me to see
opening up the vaults to reality
Hair
only for me to pull
left in the drain
to circle downwards
into a spiral of fleeting loss
We may regenerate

Colvet

We may reprocess

We may rethink

But the pain of dying alone

may never cease

to leave my neurons

leaving me

alone

...it's quiet here

Please remove your existence from my eyelids!

So I can see something else

something less traumatic

something more palatable

Of which

I may be thankful for

## *Aqueous Daydream*

The synthetic taste

of this coffee water

is starting

to disagree

with my taste buds

crack open a new drum

fresh aroma

sweeping through my nostrils

comfort

in the form of a cup

but I've cheapened out

Now

my emotional motherboard

Is short-circuiting

sparking

anxious tendencies

I'm switching to water

Aqueous Daydream

*A type of mom, I wish for*
*#1  (Daggerfall)*

I just wish

I had the type of mom

who didn't chain-smoke

to cope

which became my own cloak too

I just wish

I had the type of mom

who didn't aimlessly wander

the house for days

see anxiety

doesn't fall like an apple

rather a thousand daggers

barely piercing the skin

but enough to notice

I just wish

I had the type of mom

who didn't poke and prod

and break her vows of privacy

into the exact details of my every

move

sadly living vicariously
through my twenty-something
life cruise

I just wish
I had the type of mom
who didn't make everything
such a big deal
either it is non-existent
or an inflammatory mess
a life of pure terror

I just wish
I had the type of mom
who didn't have to gossip
and dispel detailed
intimate
personal
issues
to her supposed
friends and family

I just wish
I had the type of mom
who didn't always bear an

excuse
like her "health problems"
no matter how real or fake
preventing her
from sharing a bed
with her husband
you are sick
no doubt
maybe a warm loving
grasp
is your medicinal cure

I just wish
I had the type of mom
who could leave
a 5-10 mile radius
of her own home
in the last
30-40 years

I love you mom
I always have
you've been the only
*ounce* of support

well in terms of human contact...

but when

fucking when

will you understand

that your dagger tree

in the backyard

constantly waiting to fall

and ripen

is scaring you

preventing you

from ever moving on

and the fear

of daggerfall

has left all of those

that you love

also

constantly

anxiously

delusionally

waiting for the next pierce of skin

*out girl scouting*
When will the true witch,
Beast of the North,
hunt those who slay her kin
and detach from childhood
golden girl stories
Stop selling cookies,
start making sense

For I my dear
may never burn
since it is fire and ash
which hath created me
Purplish dyed fluids
fill the natural
nooks and crannies
of my cardboard box coated
skin
I seem flammable
but go on ahead then
try to light a spark
I **DARE** you

See

only christened demons

may emerge

from the black void

of my decaying corpse

still in death I suffer

bringing reality

finally

to those golden dipped

crystal earthbound

eyes

I'm not your enemy

but I'm not afraid

to stab back

up-stab

or down-stab

hurts all the same

No remorse

residing in my aching bones

just crunchy

crystalline

agglomerates

So go on then

Colvet

make my pores pour purple

so the singing

decrepit

lady of the lake

spirit of my desire

can burn your face to a crisp

out of tradition

not for favour

Revenge

sure is ugly ain't it?

Good thing...

really...

that I'm scum

## *Dishonest Dissonance*

In accordance with an attitude
your shambles
stiffen and break
as I climb with my tender hands
off a steep mountain
ledge
where I sit and wonder
If death may disappear
like whiteout
for ink
or pink erasers
for lead
a whispering whistling willow
designed
to bear the woes of humanity
so much life yet an appreciable
amount of death
xylem
phloem
stick and twine
stabilized in place
as I wipe away the memories

Colvet

Captivated
at the water surface
like an interface
we must not be abound
crinkling
and callowing
begging
to hear the sounds
that will place me back home

## A Filtration System

Crop dusted upon the sea level
things look different from down here
the perspective switches
perplexing the creator
upon which
only new information may be gleaned
yet the concept of creation
springing feelings
of worthlessness and uneasiness
pure abhorrence
only guided by conceptual time
existent for the sake of grounding
and tying down the articles
which yield inspiration and personality
strewn together on a canvas
displayed for others to gawk
to gasp
to misinterpret
and to skew
wiping away the water
and replacing the level with oil
too heavy to drain

too toxic to touch

Rather
are we not meager particles?

free to flow and disperse
a homogenous concoction
carefully placed
in the most tasteful of ways
yet errors pursue
and entropy dominates
offering locale
and extreme
depths of complacency
what may seem congruent
may be a mystic switch
tangled
and woven
in the earth
only left for some to see
a bandpass filter
altering the conceivable impression
of what may exist
of what may cause us pain

and of what may cause us

to be willing

to die

*Bending Physics*

The reflections

and refractions

of light

guide our eyes

appropriately

yet

we've become transfixed

almost entranced

by that

which we cannot conceive

only leaving brief reminders

memos

if you will

of how all that we may know

can be squished

and squashed

into a new product

which we are not yet prepared for

leaving us stumbling

and stalling

to search

for a final answer

## *Den of Inquiry*

Anxiously shaken

awoken and pulsating

drip

fall

tumble

trickle

and topple

over the water-bourne eardrum

which conducts

the liquid signals

into a decipherable

but tormentous sound

shackles shaking

bonds breaking

cars crushing

pavement pummeling

while we may walk with wonder

we are guided by order

consciously

waiting

a pause

an attempt

Colvet

to catch up
while it may seem simple
it is oftentimes
the difficulty which we enjoy to decipher
the mundane becomes hardened
a metamorphosis
hiding the true being
and existence
forever shining through
creating
an opaque glow
to set our unsettled hearts
free
back
into the den of
inquiry

*It's ashing*

It's ashing
on your shoes
on your socks
watching single particles
drop
in a vacuum
of hazy
cannabis
cloudy skies




Let me take myself away...

*TAN*

All I can focus on

as I walk down the funeral aisle

is one

no two

pairs of stammering eyes

I'm not in their field of vision yet

But I know they're waiting

patiently

eagerly

awaiting

to see what I've become

what little money I possess

or how messy my hair may be

or how deplorable my cracked front tooth is

these visible marks from past loves

and eyes

indicating addiction

rehab

addiction

rehab

rinse

repeat...

I'm sorry I'm not making you proud
I'm pretty battered myself
blended to a pulp
sprinkled upon
the purple poinsettias
on the priest's prying altar
I understand I am not welcome here
your house is not mine O'Lord
I belong elsewhere
I just don't know where that is quite yet

I'm trying so hard
others see it
I know for a fact
that others do
so I won't bat an eye
or turn my head
or shift my feet
to take one single glare at you
until you hand me old bank statements and junk mail

I left part of myself
in the Men's washroom
in that unfamiliar church

Colvet

amongst those brave old faces
under banishment
from future ties...
you make my body physically ache
after taking a hit
thinking
about how hollow your head must be
filled
with nothing but amyloid plaques
I know that sounds morbid
but hey
I have been hurtin' too man
and I just wanted to learn
how to be pure
.~~Mudstricken.~~

## *Pickering Fractals*

If one rock was plucked

from the precipice

of a towering display,

would the remaining rocks fall?

Or would they patiently sit

and wait

abiotically

to be plucked

on a different day?

Fractality in the slightest...

Please

don't

pluck

me

today.

## Conditional String

```
Humans='Polluting';
if Humans=='Polluting'
disp('Earthly Destruction');
else
disp('Extinction of Mankind')
end
```

## THANK YOU to:

~~drugs~~
~~alcohol~~
~~boyfriends~~
~~parents~~
~~family~~
~~friends~~
~~travelling/wandering~~
~~instructors~~
~~educators~~
~~punks~~
~~metal-heads~~
~~grinders~~
~~social media~~
~~Amazon~~
~~allpoetry.com~~
~~philosophy~~
~~Buddhism~~
~~Zen~~
~~technology~~
~~coffee~~
~~love~~
~~intellucualism~~
~~poetry~~
~~God~~
~~Satan~~
~~my therapist~~
**the reader** for saving my life.

Made in the USA
Middletown, DE
07 January 2026